Education and the Barricades

Books by Charles Frankel

EDUCATION AND THE BARRICADES
THE NEGLECTED ASPECT OF FOREIGN AFFAIRS
THE LOVE OF ANXIETY AND OTHER ESSAYS
THE DEMOCRATIC PROSPECT
THE CASE FOR MODERN MAN
THE FAITH OF REASON

Books Edited by Charles Frankel

ROUSSEAU'S SOCIAL CONTRACT
THE USES OF PHILOSOPHY: AN IRWIN EDMAN READER
ISSUES IN UNIVERSITY EDUCATION
THE GOLDEN AGE OF AMERICAN PHILOSOPHY

by Charles Frankel

Education and the Barricades

The Norton Library
W · W · NORTON & COMPANY · INC ·
NEW YORK

SBN 393-00504-6

PRINTED IN THE UNITED STATES OF AMERICA

2 3 4 5 6 7 8 9 0

To students I have known at Columbia

Contents

Foreword

LIKE MANY OTHER PROFESSORS, I have thought about the problems of higher education for most of my working life. During the past three years, however, I have had a chance to think about them from a different point of view. For most of that period I served as an official of the government, concerned with educational and cultural affairs. The experience made me realize, with more pain than I had previously felt, how little the government is doing that it ought to do for higher education, and how much of what it has done has been clumsy. It made me realize, too, how close the relationship is between great national policies and the everyday affairs of colleges and universities, and how corrosive can be the effects on the educational process of an act of national self-deception like the war in Vietnam.

But something else was driven home to me: the state of disarray of the higher educational community itself. It has been faced by new choices for which it has been ill prepared. Students, teachers, administrators are full of discontents about the present condition of higher education, and full of plans, hopes, words, and ideals intended to make things better. But serious and sustained discussion has been sporadic, and there has been too little attention to basic ideas and assumptions.

Perhaps the events which took place at Columbia, my own university, during the spring of 1968, are in part the consequence of this. While I was not present on the campus during these dramatic events, I have necessarily concerned myself with, and tried to learn about, some of the issues which require much thought, much consideration, as people at Columbia and at other institutions turn to the future. When I have touched upon the controversy at Columbia, however, it has been purely for illustrative purposes, and in pursuit of more general themes. I do not qualify as a reporter, commentator, or historian of the Columbia episode and am not passing judgment on its specific aspects.

Indeed, I have felt that my handicaps as a judge or historian of these specific events might also give me a certain advantage. The task that most needs to be done is not to distribute blame, but to separate fundamental from subordinate issues and to turn attention to general principles. There is not much point in raking over the past; thinking about the future is a much more urgent matter.

CHARLES FRANKEL

Education and the Barricades

Chapter One

The American University in Trouble

IT HAS finally come to be accepted that American colleges and universities are in trouble. The questions about them mount in number: Who is to blame for the disruptions and ugly incidents that have left American campuses disturbed? Is it the students? The administrations? The police? Could these upsetting events have been avoided? Is there only one side to the story, or two, or three? Why are the young so angry, and what do they want anyway? Why are the old so dim-witted, and why do they resist change and progress? But the answers to these questions will not tell us what is wrong with American higher education, or what principles should be employed in setting about to improve it.

No reforms can be discussed intelligently or responsibly unless we take the phrases that now dominate discussion—"student rights," "student power," "participation," "democracy," "a relevant education," and all the rest—and ask seriously what they mean, and what assumptions are behind them. Is higher education an egalitarian enterprise? Are the principles of democracy applicable to it? What do we mean by these principles anyway? Do students have a right to demand power? Are colleges and universities political institutions like other political institutions? Are students an interest-group, like organized labor? And what about illegality as a political tactic? Is it ever permissible? When? And does it make no difference whether it takes place on a university campus or not? Unless we think about such issues, the discussion of higher education and its problems remains merely impressionistic.

The present essay is an effort to consider these fundamental questions. Students, teachers, administrators, trustees, and the general public are now finally thinking in something like a concerted way about the condition of American colleges and universities. In doing so, the need is to think not only about how these institutions ought to be governed, but about what the proper order of things in a college or university should be. Indeed, this process of thought has implications that go beyond education. The issues that have been raised on American campuses touch on matters of broad significance for American life as a whole—the role of the young, the relation of the citizen to authority, the position of the individual in large collectivities, the growing alienation of educated people, the significance of words like "liberty" and "equality."

Columbia, Michigan State, Northwestern, Stanford, are only where the lightning has happened to strike. The disorders on these campuses are reflections in part of disorders in the larger society—disorders in our social arrangements, and disorders in the ways in which we think about these arrangements. This is not the first time that dissatisfaction with education has reflected a breakdown in prevailing intellectual and moral codes. And so in asking where American education ought to go from here, we are also asking, at least in part, where American thinking and American society ought to go from here.

Obviously, this brief essay does not provide an answer to such far-reaching questions. But perhaps it will help provoke an orderly discussion of them.

Chapter Two

Why Little Beginnings
Have Large Results

IT WOULD BE BEST to begin by trying to take our bearings and to see things in their true proportions. Is American higher education in as bad a way as the tensions which have broken loose on campuses throughout the country would appear to suggest? Granted that the demonstrations which initiate these episodes are usually started by small groups of students whose political opinions place them at the fringes of the student body. And granted, too, that there are bound to be a certain number of such students on every reasonably diversified campus. Still, how does it happen that, as events unfold, these people who seem to be at the extremes attract so many adherents? Why do they appear to make sense to larger numbers of other students, to more members of the faculty, and to a wider public than most of us would have supposed beforehand?

The answer to this question is an introduction into one

of the perennial miracles of history—the way in which minorities suddenly become majorities, the way in which unpopular ideas become popular. Real facts, real grievances, are usually at the kernel. But these are then wrapped inside powerful conventions and stereotypes, which give them a larger size and a higher sheen. Into this compound are poured loyalties to class or group or generation. And then these facts and grievances are linked to the worst follies and injustices of society. Thus, random and scattered discontents are brought together, and specific demands for specific reforms turn suddenly into revolutionary manifestos. This is what has happened on American campuses. American higher education has real and serious faults. But much of what has happened has little to do with higher education's inadequacies. It has been a reaction to the world beyond the cloister. Although the situations at particular colleges and universities differ, certain general propositions apply to all or most of them, and explain, I believe, why campus disturbances have shown such a remarkable tendency to mushroom.

We have to begin with a fact that is likely to characterize any intellectually interesting campus: in any such setting, a latent predisposition in favor of turning things upside down is present. All lively and well-informed professors cast doubt, simply in the normal course of their teaching, on things that the conventional pieties take for granted. And students are ready to make as much of this as they can. They are immersed in the process of defining their identities and their relation to the world, and they make special demands upon the world. They want it to be *theirs*: they want a piece of its action, they want it to meet their standards of what is decent and just, they want to test themselves in it.

Accordingly, allies are present, potentially, for almost

any program of rebellion, whatever its specific cause or ultimate rationale. Give students a movement which makes the right sounds—against racism, against napalm, against bigness and materialism and bureaucracy—and a large number will be willing at least to listen sympathetically. Challenge them to take a stand, to get off the fence, and they will begin to stir uncomfortably. Turn the police on the demonstrators, whether with or without good reason, and this sympathy and this discomfort will turn to active support. Attempt to punish some of the participants, and feelings of group solidarity and collective grievance will be further strengthened. And much of this is true for faculty members too, particularly the younger ones. There are phrases that have almost the same whiplash effect in faculty meetings that "Uncle Tom" does in civil rights circles: one of them is "ivory tower," another is "pro-administration."

Nor is this all. Today, these stirrings take place within a culture that has unusual features. By and large, colleges and universities are part of what has come to be known as "liberal culture." And this culture does not react to conflicts between the young and the old as most other cultures have. It does not take in stride the young who buck against the process of being brought up, of being taught how to behave and what to think. It does not think of them as naturally unruly animals, still too unformed to know what is good for them. On the contrary, it is embarrassed by conflicts between the young and the "old," and it tends to put the burden of proof on the old. It would like to believe that if the old only did things right there would be no conflicts. In our novels and plays, in our educational philosophy, in our psychoanalytic theories, the adult is regularly cast in the role of villain. He is always the enemy of youthful honesty and natural instincts, always the opponent of that process of purification and resurrection which it is the eternal role of youth to bring about. Even when he is presented sympathetically, it is in the role of slow learner.

There is, of course, some truth in these conventions: they are no worse, certainly, than the paternalistic and authoritarian conventions that they replaced. The young do tend to have a fresher and richer sense of possibility; and where social and moral issues are concerned, their sensibilities have not been rubbed smooth by habit, routine, and accommodation. Still, there is also, fairly obviously, a certain amount of pure fiction in these conventions. Everyone has known young hypocrites, and young careerists. And young fanatics can suffer from stiffening of the brain just as bad as any elderly bureaucrat's. But while these facts are known, this knowledge tends to be suppressed. When the virtues of youth are celebrated, most people, particularly in liberal middle-class circles, hesitate to express even a modicum of skepticism. For such skepticism challenges feelings as old as Christianity, as recent as progressive education, and as basic as our love of our children. Besides, disapproval of the young suggests that you're growing old, which is something that most people hate to admit.

Thus, the dice tend to be loaded when an administration becomes embroiled in a struggle with students. The onlookers bring certain conditioned reflexes to the spectacle. Young people look good fighting for a new order of things. We forgive them their trespasses, literally and figuratively. We forgive them their impatience and their callow ideas. In contrast, if a university administrator shows irritation, he seems puffy or faintly comic. And if he goes so far as to insist that in fulfillment of his obligation to restore orderly procedures, he must call the police, he is put down as an authoritarian who prefers *force majeure* to conducting a "dialogue." The young people spill their own blood in the struggle. The old call in the cops to do their dirty work. The situation is too uncomfortably reminiscent of the division of labor in war. So allies for the students mount.

And then, of course, there are also the objective realities. These make the older people look bad too. American colleges and universities have been short-changing their students for years. The American undergraduate has usually made a grinding effort to be accepted in college. When he gets there, he may very well feel that he is in an institution where the classes are large, the minds of the instructors small, and the only sense of a collective institutional purpose comes from the clicking of the I.B.M. machines. Much college teaching is indifferent or incompetent. Courses are marked by a sickly specialism not clearly related to any identifiable goals of liberal education, and remote from the problems on the student's mind. Boards of trustees seem either not to know what's going on or not to care. And administrations seem stiff, mechanical, impersonal, and out of touch with basic facts of life. If only to give themselves a sense of community, many students will be sympathetic to collective efforts, however disruptive, to get these authorities' attention and wake them up.

And yet, although the colleges have their faults, they also have enough virtues to make life within them quite bearable. American scholarship is productive and sophisticated, college life has intrinsic attractions, and students, after all, are in the right situation and at the right age to keep one another amused, instructed and stimulated. The largest factor in student discontent comes from off the campus. A study by the American Council of Education has indicated that of 71 campus disturbances since October, 1966, 68 were related either to civil rights questions or the war. Colleges and universities, given the people who inhabit them, are simply sensitive barometers of the general social weather.

College students today are confronted by the prospect of participating in a war in which a very large number of them passionately disbelieve. The best people in their generation, and the people they admire most in the generations ahead of them, have protested for years. The protests have had little effect. It should not be surprising that, for so many of the members of the present college generation, rage should be a constant emotion, on the surface or just below it. What is surprising, indeed, is the number of people in this generation who are reasonably good-tempered. The sympathies of many of the young naturally go out to those who, through one action or another, are trying to make the people in charge of this country stop and listen. The sympathies of a great many of their elders, after all, are not different. And if the dramatic actions that are taken include disrupting a university, it can perhaps be expected that young people will contemplate this tactic with somewhat less sense of moral outrage than those who are not of draft age.

Nor can they be expected to be all eyes and ears in listening to lectures on the evils of force and violence. The young are particularly alert to inconsistency and hypocrisy. They cannot help but note that student radicals are not alone in what they say or in what they do with regard to violence. The government of the United States has also been prepared to sacrifice good and urgent purposes in order to pursue a policy of ascending violence; its justification for doing so has also been fuzzy and abstract, not to say romantic and impractical; and it too has obstinately persisted in this course in the face of all objections that there must be a more peaceful way.

Of course, none of these observations prove that what students have done in response to their feelings has been right. That remains an open question. The actions of student demonstrators, and the support they have received from other students and from professors and part of the public, may be irrational and wrong—excessive, aimed at the wrong target, injurious to fundamental values that any responsible man ought to keep in his mind. To understand why people have the feelings they do, and to feel some sympathy with them, is not to say that their behavior is justified. Justified or not, however, the student demonstrations during the spring of 1968 were responses to irritations that are serious and of long standing. And it is these irritations that mainly explain why the demonstrations have been supported by large numbers of students not normally militant.

Indeed, college students' grievances about the war are no longer abstract or postponable issues. The recently enacted changes in the draft law have made them immediate and personal. The combination of a misconceived war and a foolish draft law has achieved a result which most informed observers of the American scene would have thought impossible a few short years ago. It has converted American students into something like an interest-group with a common grievance and has given large numbers of them a sense of sharing a common practical destiny with other aggrieved and exploited groups. In a word, it has pushed American student politics closer to the student politics of the poorer countries.

What has been taking place on American campuses, in fact, is simply the reflection, in a peculiarly sensitive mirror, of the larger crisis affecting American society. An unpersuaded people has been asked to sacrifice too much, including conscience, for a cruel and unintelligible war. Too many words have been spoken, too many promises made, too little action taken, with regard to civil rights, the misery in our cities, and the implausible conception of human priorities reflected in our foreign policy and our national budget. Moreover, the sacrifice has been unequal, which aggravates the difficulties in a time of war. Some families have known stark tragedy; many people have known uneasiness and bitterness; but many, too, have been able to half-forget the war, feeling it only in the form of taxes they can afford. And as a consequence, the credit on which our system draws when it asks for allegiance, the reservoir of trust and confidence into which a government dips when it asks for obedience to law and order, are leaking away. We are living through the deepest kind of political crisis—what can be called a "crisis of legitimacy." It is not possible to insulate universities from such a crisis—universities least of all: they have usually been the first places to register the existence of such a crisis.

There is at least a possibility of dealing with the crisis, however, and, in doing so, of moving forward. Crises of legitimacy are broadly of two kinds. One is the crisis that is caused when the standards by which the existing regime justifies its existence are challenged by rival standards. This is the kind of crisis that Christianity created for the Roman Empire, or that the democratic ideas of Rousseau represented to the Old Regime in France. In contrast, the second kind of crisis of legitimacy comes when a society fails to legitimate itself in its own terms, when it fails to do what its own rationale calls for it to do. The present situation obviously contains elements of both kinds of crisis, but it still remains primarily a crisis of the second kind. People are not attacking the ideals of democracy. They are not saying that government by the consent of the governed is a foolish or wicked idea. On the contrary, wisely or not, they are asking for more of it than they now have.

This represents a situation in which a sense of authority and direction can be restored if the right actions are taken. In this respect, the fundamental crisis in our universities is a political crisis which is part of a larger political crisis in the country, and part of the political crisis, indeed, that has touched practically every other developed country east and west of the Elbe. Governments today share one thing in common: the people they are governing don't seem to appreciate them. In all these countries a new kind of politics has arisen, different from the old and bewildering to the oldsters. People want more freedom, people want more power, but their politics is not simply a politics of grievances, a politics for repairing definite wrongs. Malaise, alienation, generalized disapproval are also involved. They arise from the feeling that hypocrisy is in the saddle, that the quality of life is debased, and that people do not have the kind of control over their lives that their indoctrination in the philosophy of democracy has told them they should have.

It is this demand for power and participation, this demand that somehow the processes of communication and control by which citizens keep governments responsive be repaired, that marks the new politics, here and in other countries, in universities and outside them. This explains, I think, why so much of the emphasis in the more radical forms of the new politics is on means rather than ends, on action rather than goals. What is it that the students want? goes the question. It is a fair question, and the answer is indefinite. But the reason it is indefinite is that the activists among the students do not want any particular thing: they want the feel of power; they want access to it; they want it in the bank so they can get what they want just in case they can decide what it is they do want.

Perhaps all of this makes sense; perhaps some of it does; perhaps none. But certain things are plain. Plainest of all is the fact that in discussing university difficulties and university reform we are not discussing only higher education. The principles at issue affect the citizen's relation to government, the fundamental social experiences of subordination and super-ordination, and the very spirit and quality of personal relations. It is not hard to understand, therefore, why small issues on a campus take on major dimensions. Nor is it hard to understand why small groups pick up major support. What is happening in universities reflects a drastic change in the political climate. Things are going to have to be different in universities, and things are likely to be different in the world at large.

Chapter Three

Thoughts for the Barricades or for Education?

IN WHAT WAY are things going to have to be different in universities? It is astonishing how little genuine public discussion there has been of this question, how little of what has been said has gone beneath the surface of slogan and generality. People have lined up to show their sympathies—their "liberalism" or "conservatism" in politics, their "progressive" or "traditionalist" views in education. They have used words to show on which side of the barricades their loyalties lie. But little has been said that suggests that possibly the answers do not all fall neatly on one side of the fence or the other. It is remarkable how many learned men there are, men who enjoy the ambiguities of John Donne's poetry or who spend their lives refining the refinements of Wittgenstein's philosophy, who nevertheless sail into the middle of social controversies with all their answers ready and all their powers of qualified judgment put aside.

The discussion of the reform of American higher education is a discussion of something important. Statements of one's sympathy for youthful idealism, or of one's belief in the validity of democracy in all domains of life, do little to illuminate the issues. It takes no great wit, and no recent immersion in "the politics of confrontation," to recognize that the destiny of universities is not shaped by intellectual considerations alone. Still, universities have something to do with the life of the mind. If we are going to envisage reshaping them, it seems relevant to look at the issues as though they presented intellectual problems. Designing a university is not, after all, a form of action-painting.

Nor is it a matter of setting forth broad general principles and reasoning deductively from them, so that one is invariably in favor of "student power" or opposed to it, on the side of "university democracy" or against it. General principles are relevant to what one thinks about such matters, but specific problems differ, and the application of these general principles, in consequence, cannot always be the same. That is where the rub is, and that is where serious intellectual examination of the issues really begins.

THE OBVIOUS PLACE to begin is with the concept of "student power." What does the phrase mean?

Before we talk about the reforms for which the phrase stands, we should recognize that it gives a good description of a fact that has long existed. Undoubtedly "student power" is the name of something new and important and debatable—indeed, it is the name of several different things which have to be separated one from the other. But "student power" also calls for something neither quite so radical as its more ardent devotees appear to think, nor so arrogant and opposed to the natural order of things as its angrier opponents seem to feel. It is, to begin with, simply a new name for perhaps the dominant fact about higher education as an everyday process.

This fact is that students are not only the objects of education, but its principle instruments. An institution and its faculty can provide facilities, stimulation, some guidance and orientation, a sense of standards and of models to emulate. But the primary environment for the student is other students. They set the pace for one another; they have more to do than any other group in the university with what the student pays attention to from day to day; they do much of the teaching that counts.

Moreover, students also have great influence on the evolution of educational theory and practice. They have not, in the past, voted on curricula or met with the faculty in formal sessions. Just the same, they have had an effect, like the effect of the climate, on curriculum, the character of the teaching staff, the rules of campus life, and the composition of future student bodies. General education was for a long time, for example, an exciting and viable part of the curricula of many undergraduate institutions. Increasingly, over the past decade or so, there have been countercurrents. And the largest reason has been that students changed. They came to college differently and better prepared than their predecessors, or with more highly developed interests in specializing, or with greater impatience to get on to vocationally useful subjects. The colleges have responded to these new attitudes because inattention or resistance in the classroom requires a response.

Similar changes have occurred in other areas, also as a result of student opinion. The movement towards coeducation has accelerated; the idea of a year at work, or a year abroad, or a year simply to pause and rethink what one is doing at college in the first place, has become increasingly acceptable; the rules governing life in dormitories have been greatly altered. There are, in fact, not many educational practices with regard to which students have had strong and focused opinions which have not felt the influence of these opinions.

Students exercise this influence, in the first place, simply because they are the most numerous group on the campus, and teachers and administrators, much as they may prefer not to, have to live with them. No educational program will work if students will not let it. They do not have to demonstrate against it. They simply have to submit to it passively and unexcitedly. Higher education is an accommodative process; it doesn't take if teachers and administrators talk down to students or talk past them. Students, therefore, always have a kind of residual power over their educational experience. This is true no matter how an institution is organized, or what it imagines its philosophy of education to be.

Moreover, students have a second weapon in their arsenal. American higher education gives them consumer's choice. They can choose among teachers, among different programs of study, among different institutions. Through these choices they encourage one kind of development and discourage another. They shape the distribution of the university's resources, and they create in it a style, an emphasis on some things and a neglect of others, which helps lure future students to it and push other potential students away. Thus, the student's choices are the student's votes. They contribute, even if unintentionally, to the general course of evolution of an institution of learning.

The power that students have should not, of course, be exaggerated. It works slowly. It is small comfort to a young man or woman to know that, four or five years after he or she has left the university, the dear, slow thing will catch on and mend its ways. And not only is the power that students have slow in achieving an effect, but it is limited. Other sources of power and influence work on a university, as they should, and students do not get everything they want, even slowly. Yet the influence of students, limited though it may be, is nevertheless real and significant. If one has a long enough time-span in mind, students exercise an influence as large as any other group's in bringing about alterations in higher education.

Thus, the question raised by present demands for student power is not really whether students should finally be given the right to say something about what happens to them. It is whether it would be educationally desirable to create arrangements permitting students to participate more visibly and formally in the making of educational decisions. Considered as a general proposition, there can be little doubt, I think, that this is the direction in which change should proceed. And the reason is not only that, for better or worse, the rising moral sentiment in the world at large is in favor of giving more independence and power to the young, and the college and university cannot hold out indefinitely against this process. (Indeed, if this is the wrong direction in which to go, perhaps colleges and universities should try to resist it.) The more important reasons are drawn from both educational and democratic theory. If people have some power over the way in which they live and work, they have more interest in their experience, and they learn more from it. If they have some power, they tend to become more responsible. They are more likely to make the connections between ideas and action, rhetoric and reality, that are at once the tests and the pleasures of the moral life. These propositions have been tried in other fields and found to have a substantial amount of truth in them. They have not been tried to the extent that they could be in higher education.

But these are generalities, precisely the kind against which I railed earlier. They tell us about a desirable direction of change. They do not tell us how far the change should go, or if there are any areas in which it should not take place at all. When we get down to brass tacks, what can "student power" mean?

Should students, for example, participate in the selection and promotion of members of the faculty? When they think a good teacher has been fired, they certainly have a right to complain. When faculty members treat them as odd and anonymous objects, to be avoided whenever possible, they have a right to demand the services for which they or the community are paying. Students do not have, in most American universities, the ways and means to assert these rights in an effective and orderly fashion. That situation requires repair. But students nevertheless cannot have a formal role in the selection of faculty.

The reasons against granting such a right are numerous. Good teaching is not a matter of majority vote; as in wine, women, and song, tastes differ. A good teacher for a small group may be an ineffective teacher for large numbers. In addition, students cannot always judge good teaching; they often discover a man's merits or demerits only years after they have left his class.

Students, furthermore, cannot make informed judgments about aspects of a man's performance which are indispensable to determining whether he is a good teacher. They can judge whether he is intelligible, stimulating, sympathetic, but not whether he is giving them the best informa-

tion available, or organizes his materials as a competent prac-
titioner of his discipline should. Only other members of the
faculty can judge that. And students, of course, see only
one part of the teaching process. There are people on every
faculty whose best students are other faculty members.
They themselves may not communicate well with the
young, but they are sources of insight and excitement to
their colleagues, and that insight and excitement is trans-
mitted to students. Good teaching is the product not simply
of individual talent, but of the quality of an entire intellectual community. Nor is teaching the only function of a professor. He has other duties, and his colleagues have to judge
how well he performs them.

But the most important reason why student power cannot extend to the selection of faculty is that this would be
incompatible with academic freedom. It exposes the teacher
to intimidation. Academic freedom is the product of a long
and difficult struggle. It has been achieved by excluding all
groups but professors from any formal power over what
goes on in the classroom. The exclusion applies to administrators, trustees, legislators, parents, alumni, and the public.
There are questions that can be asked about academic freedom—about its range and extent, about misinterpretations
of it, about departures from it that have been defended in
its name—but there are no reasons for reconsidering the role
of students in relation to it. There is nothing about students
to justify giving them a power no other group has.

Students have no common professional perspective or
shared occupational interest in academic freedom. Judging
from the record, numbers of them are subject to the same
bouts of intolerance in the face of upsetting ideas that affect
bankers or legislators. A wise faculty and administration will
do well to try to find out what student opinions about teach-

ers are. But they had better conduct the canvass informally and discreetly. Teaching is a professional relationship, not a popularity contest. To invite students to participate in the selection or promotion of their teachers is to create a relationship in the classroom inappropriate to teaching.

Should students have the right to demand the introduction of certain courses? Again, there are limits. The fact that students want a course is a reason to consider giving it. But it is not, by itself, a sufficient reason. There may be nobody competent to teach the course. It may be a non-course—an excuse for bull sessions on company time, with no literature worth studying and no tradition of discourse and inquiry to hold things in bounds. Besides, since university budgets have been known to be limited, there is always the disagreeable possibility that the introduction of a new course requires the dropping of an old one. A judgment of comparative worth therefore has to be made. Students are not the right jury to make such a judgment.

Yet these arguments merely define the limits of student power. They do not argue against it. On the contrary, the advantages of having students make recommendations on curriculum are considerable. Students have things to teach their teachers. And there are invaluable things they can learn about their education, about universities, about themselves, from taking part in the examination, with their teachers, of the design of their education. Moreover, the entire spirit within an institution of learning is likely to be better if there is a sense within it that its members are constantly cooperating in the appraisal of what it is doing. There ought to be regular, established procedures for consultation between faculties and student bodies. They should provide for the genuine, serious, and continuing examination of curriculum—a process incompatible with mass meetings, demonstrations, and sloganeering. It should not be expected that all student recommendations be accepted, but it should be expected that the consideration of students' points of view will not be merely *pro forma*.

Such arrangements would have a number of merits, not least among them the possibility that a myth generally accepted by students would finally be exploded. Students might discover that on many issues, particularly those directly related to courses and curriculum, it is not professors but deans and presidents who are their natural allies. By and large, judging from my own experience, it is members of the faculty, and not administrators, who are the opponents of educational reforms. This is not because deans and presidents are naturally more liberal. It is simply because most men's recognition of the need for reform grows in direct proportion to the distance of the proposed reform from their own territory. If students are talking about the reform of the curriculum, they will probably find more sympathy among deans, who don't work in classrooms. If students have complaints about the food served in dining halls, they will probably find the most sympathetic listeners, on the other hand, among members of the faculty. Professors don't have to balance the budget or hire the cooks.

BUT LET US TURN to the administrator's territory—to matters ranging from the government of residence halls through student discipline to the major decisions, which administrators and trustees make, regarding the allocation of the university's resources and its relations to government, the economy, and the surrounding community. How far should we go with "student power" in this domain?

Once again, the question is begged unless we look at it, first and foremost, from an educational point of view. Consider residence halls. There are colleges where students, with minor exceptions, are required to live in residence halls. Let us suppose, for purposes of argument, that a majority of students are opposed to this requirement. There is still no absolute requirement to accept this verdict of the student majority. For to go by "majority rule" is to miss the point. A rule that students must live on campus reflects the belief that students benefit from living together in an academic environment. This is an educational theory. It may be a foolish one, and it certainly is not true for all students. But this does not mean that a majority vote of students justifies its rejection. For no student has to accept this theory. He can choose a college where living in dormitories is optional, or no dormitories exist at all.

The crucial right that is at stake in this and comparable matters is neither students' freedom to choose their own way of life, nor students' right to govern themselves democratically through majority rule. The first of these rights is protected by the existence of choice between different institutions; the second right is inapplicable, first because students are on a campus only briefly, and cannot be given the power to dismantle arrangements about which future generations of students may have different opinions, and, second, because there is another right at stake which annuls the claim of a majority to have its way. This right is the right of different institutions to follow their own ideas; it is the community's right to enjoy the benefits of educational pluralism and experimentation. Majority rule has no standing here, just as it has no standing with respect to the existence of minority religions or unpopular political creeds.

Nor does this deprive students of effective power. A college that insists on campus residence may well find that, as the years pass, it is losing the kind of student it would like to have. It will then have to ask itself how much of a price it wishes to pay to maintain this part of its educational program. This has been happening to colleges hitherto opposed to coeducation. The change in student outlook is the largest single factor in the present drift towards universal coeducation at the undergraduate level. But this response has been the free choice of the college authorities involved. Their right to choose freely is the key right in this context, so long as students have the complementary right to choose one kind of college or another.

Similarly, the role that should properly be assigned to students in the government of residence halls is also a matter not of basic student rights, but of what is best educationally. Since students differ, there is no universal formula. As a general rule, the maximum amount of self-government in dormitories is probably desirable, but here too there are limitations. A university has educational purposes, and it maintains residence halls as instruments in the accomplishment of these purposes. Students cannot be permitted to make decisions or take actions incompatible with these educational objectives. Moreover, a university has obligations to the laws of the larger community. It exists under these laws, and its charter derives from them. It can only maintain its rights to police itself if its facilities are used in accordance with these laws. Student self-government in dormitories is desirable, but university authorities must therefore retain a residual right of veto.

In fact, the operative questions are not the broad theoretical ones about students' rights, but the practical, bread-and-butter questions. Are dormitory facilities bad? Are dining halls adequate? Are fees exorbitant? When we speak of "student power" in connection with living arrangements on a campus, the key matter is the existence of formal procedures for airing grievances about such matters. Not enough institutions of learning have such procedures. This is where the fault is, and not in the differences between life in dormitories and life in a rooming-house.

What about the administration of student discipline? Should this be "democratized"? If so, what does this mean? Because there has been struggle and confrontation between different groups inside universities, the question of student discipline is currently being approached primarily from a political and legal point of view. The issues have been formulated in terms of the fair distribution of power, the balancing of the claims of the different parties at conflict, and the protection of the rights of students. And so the most usual formula proposed has been the creation of joint faculty-student committees.

In the present atmosphere, this is probably the right direction in which to move. In large, impersonal institutions, subject to massive pressures from the outside, students ought to have protection when they get into trouble with the system. They ought to have the right to be judged, at their request, by their teachers and their peers. This is all the more important because the phrase "student discipline" is now likely to include a new kind of problem—infractions of rules for political or moral reasons. These are not the old-fashioned problems which the traditional disciplinary codes were created to handle. They raise special questions of rights, and of representation of the various groups concerned. The reasons for dealing with them by procedures in which students and faculty are participants, therefore, are persuasive. If suspicion, rightly or wrongly, exists on a campus, it is politically desirable to assure fair and representative disciplinary proceedings from which no group has been shut out. Student participation in the administration of discipline helps remove from discipline the quality of an edict handed down by alien rulers from on high.

But in saying this, it is also important to realize that while we are speaking about the most conspicuous kinds of disciplinary issue, we are also speaking about the exceptional kinds. Student participation in the ordinary administration of discipline is not a good idea. It may even be doubtful that faculty participation is. For "discipline," in a college or university, is not normally a judicial but an educational matter. Its basic concern is not "the rights" of the student, which are not usually at issue. Its basic concern is to deal with the student's problems, and to help him along with his education. The immediate and most pressing requirement is that of establishing communication and understanding. The context is not punitive; it is therapeutic. In such a context, the adversary procedures of the courtroom or the legislative chamber are not productive. When student rights are conceived to be the only considerations, student discipline is ripped out of its educational setting.

In most normal disciplinary cases, the heart of the problem lies in essentially personal and private concerns of the student. It may be difficult or quite improper for him to talk to other students about these concerns, but it is helpful for him to talk to a dean. Most so-called problems of discipline have in fact been handled in this way in most traditional colleges. The record is not so bad that we should automatically conclude that formal judicial machinery is preferable, in normal matters of discipline, to an intelligent, humane dean working in the privacy of his office.

Moreover, it is important, also, to guard an important aspect of desirable student-teacher relationships. The relationship between teacher and student is a subtle one; it is less cluttered if the behavior of students outside the classroom is none of the teacher's business, unless students ask him to make it so. When the teacher-student relationship becomes personal, it is best that this happen as the result of a voluntary choice on both sides. This is why doubts are in order about the wisdom of bringing faculty members into everyday student disciplinary procedures. If teachers are required to take part in such procedures, this involves them, involuntarily, in the lives of their students outside the classroom. Colleges differ with regard to this matter, some bringing faculty members into the disciplinary process and some not. It would be desirable to compare the results of different systems. The everyday administration of discipline is an educational matter, to be settled by empirical observation of the facts, and clarification of educational values. It is not the kind of question that should be answered in terms of abstract formulae about the advantages of "democracy."

In sum, there is much to be said for "student power," but not the kind of thing that has brought people to the barricades. "Student power" stands for grievance procedures, where these are needed; it stands for assurances that students' rights will be respected; it stands for powers of self-government, in strictly student areas, and subject to certain residual rights of veto by an administration or a faculty; it stands for the participation by students in a continuing process of consultation with their teachers about the character and content, and the whys and wherefores, of their education. But it does not stand for any wholesale formula, like universal love or teetotalism or vegetarianism, to be adopted without interpretation or qualification no matter what the subject is.

Indeed, its most important meaning lies beyond anything that can be written down in the form of specific rules. "Student power" asks for something that does not really require the rewriting of university statutes or bylaws, and without which all such efforts to "restructure" universities will be largely futile. It calls for a change in attitude, a change in the order of priorities implicitly accepted by the members of a university in their day's work. Interpreted as an educational idea, "student power" stands for a spirit of consultation and cooperation between faculty and students, and between administrators and students. It asks professors to recognize that they are members of a community, a community with an educational purpose, and that they have responsibilities to it. It asks administrators to recognize that they should be, first and foremost, teachers and educators. One solid educational result of the recent troubles on American campuses will have been achieved when the top administrators in institutions of learning take it as part of their normal routine to sit down with students, to talk to them and listen to them. "Student power" can mean even more than bringing administration back to the students. It can mean bringing administrators back to them.

Indeed, why should not presidents and deans, as normal matters, discuss history or architecture with students? Student grievances should not be the only matters that bring students and administrators together, and a man can govern a university more judiciously if he himself engages, at least a little, in its main business, which is teaching. Admittedly, this is to propose something difficult and even revolutionary. To put it into effect would require the replacement of some top administrators, and the re-education of many others. They have been away from teaching too long, and they have been spending their time with too narrow a portion of the human race.

But there is much that these men do, and which the world expects them to do, including the raising of money, which can be done by vice-presidents and vice-deans. Or perhaps universities should have a chairman of the board who is a full-time officer of the university, and does what the university president now does. The university president, in contrast, would act as the leader of the faculty and the center of the educational community. Certainly, universities would seem less like factories, and the stereotyped antagonisms between faceless entities—"students," "faculty," "administration"—that now mar them would be less conspicuous, if administrators indicated more frequently that their own personal order of priorities, their own scheme of enjoyment and accomplishment, belonged to the same universe of discourse as that of professors and serious students. "Student power" is a demand for a change in climate as much as for a change in mechanisms. It means a different and livelier spirit of communication between the different groups that compose our institutions of higher learning.

But we have not yet discussed the largest single demand implicit in slogans like "student power" and "university democracy." This is the claim that faculty and students ought to share with trustees and administrators, or take over altogether, the powers which these latter groups have hitherto exercised alone. This is a subject which requires us to look at the political framework of institutions of learning.

Chapter Four

The Structure
of Universities

THE CLAIM that students should participate in the major decision-making processes of colleges or universities is a political one. Its justification, if it has any, is the same as that which lies behind the demand of subordinate groups who constitute a majority in other domains of society to have a say about the conditions of their life and work. The justification, in short, is the general one that democratic principles call for the establishment of student power in higher education.

But is this what "democratic principles" do entail? Indeed, do they apply to institutions of learning? Are colleges and universities sufficiently like cities or national governments, or unions or factories, to justify the use of the same political arguments in relation to them? Or are they so different that a different set of principles applies to them, in part or in whole?

Weaving through most demands for "student power," or, for that matter, some demands for "faculty power," there are recurrent assumptions. They are worth listing.

1) A university consists of separate groups or blocs. Administrators and trustees form one bloc, the faculty a second, the students a third. The relationships between these blocs are essentially like the relationships between other groups in a political situation. Power is the name of the game, and each fights to get a larger share of it. If justice is to be served, therefore, the subordinate groups have to fight for more power. In a university, this means that faculty and students form a natural alliance. They are, in effect, the workers and peasants of the university, facing its entrenched ruling class, the trustees, together with their paid lackeys, the administrators.

2) Universities are not democratic organizations, but they should be. It is a sign of the hypocrisy of present-day society that it talks about individual rights and majority rule but denies the members of the largest group in the universities—the students—any voice in their government.

3) Accordingly, government by a board of trustees, supported by an administration, must be abolished or radically altered. Students and professors should make the major decisions, and the administration should be reduced to doing the housework. At the very least, trustees and administrators should be forced to share their power. For it is not clear what trustees do, or why they have any rights over a university.

All of these assumptions have an initial plausibility about them. Yet the first, it seems to me, is a portrait of a university painted with an axe. The second is a tangle of laudable ideals and loose political philosophy. As for the third, it makes some interesting practical recommendations that are worth discussing. But if we are going to pursue them, it is important to do so for the right reasons, and most of the reasons that are given are wrong.

There are, of course, some characteristics of "class conflict" within universities. Professors bargain for their salaries with administrators. The general level of faculty salaries is influenced by pressures from the faculty. Conditions of work, such as the number of courses taught, are subjects of negotiation. The faculty as a group maintains a watchful eye over the administration to be sure that it does not trample on the faculty's rights. Professors think that administrators don't know what's going on. Administrators think that professors don't understand them. All of this resembles an employer-employee relationship.

Yet the resemblance is limited, and if it is taken as the clue to the essential nature of the relationship between faculty and administration, it is violently misleading. The professor has tenure: after he has passed certain signposts, he cannot be fired from his job short of misconduct, and not always then. His equity in his job is as firm as if he had bought it. And the president of his university can give him fewer orders about what to do with his job than his town council can give him about what to do with his house and land.

There is a fundamental respect in which the administrators of a university are in a different position from the managers of a company. The university administrators cannot create a total plan of work, define jobs within it, and then assign individual workers to them. Of course, now that labor unions have the power they have, managers cannot do this as easily as they once could. But the difference between their position and that of university administrators is nevertheless very great. The product of a factory is a corporate product to which individuals contribute. The product of a university is many separate, individual products, for which the corporate arrangements provide protection and support, but for which the individuals have basic responsibility.

The university adminstrator, by and large, has to deal with people who are intent on their own work, who have bargaining power in their own individual right, who have entrenched positions and feudal retainers around them, and who carry with them bundles of traditional freedoms and antique privileges on which they can call in time of trouble. Usually, it's no contest: the administrator is out of his league. By cajolery, by the allocation of funds, every once in a while by the power of his ideas, he can try to bring some system and purpose into the division of faculty labor. But he doesn't run the plant. This is a reason, perhaps it is the most important reason, why students so often fail to get a fair shake educationally. Universities are intensely individualistic in their structure and spirit. It is not impossible but it is difficult to bring the individualists that compose them together to study and agree on their collective business.

In brief, a university, though a hierarchy, is a discontinuous hierarchy. The faculty is one hierarchy, the administration another, and the two hierarchies do different things, generally speaking. Where their activities overlap or conflict, there has to be a settlement. But on the whole, universities manage to keep going because each group recognizes its place. The relation between administration and faculty is not a relation between superiors and subordinates, and certainly not a relation between employer and employees. It is a constitutional arrangement for the separation of powers.

The model of employer-employee relations, with its overtones of "class conflict," probably applies best, indeed, not to the relations between administration and faculty, but to the relations between senior professors and junior members of the teaching staff. Here some of the traditional—indeed, the nineteenth-century—powers of the boss over the worker apply. The junior teacher's assignment is given to him, and he depends on his boss for his bread and career. Because there has been a shortage of labor in the academic market-place in recent years, junior teachers have a somewhat better bargaining position than they once did. Nevertheless, the young instructor or professor without tenure is the closest thing we have, in a contemporary American university, to the old-fashioned exploited worker.

Where, then, do students fit into this situation? The fact is that there is no analogy from any other human collectivity that quite applies to their position in a university. Consumer, worker, recipient of favors, protected son—the student is all of these, and none. He is a consumer, yes, but an unlucky one: he has to pass tests laid down by the seller before he is allowed to leave with the prize he came to purchase. Is he a worker? There are similarities. He has to submit to the rules and regulations of the management, and produce what it wants him to produce. But he does not turn over what he produces and get a wage in return. What he produces—certain skills and attitudes, a demonstrated mastery of a field of knowledge, a set of qualities of mind he did not have when he entered—these are his, not the management's, and they are presumably for his principal benefit, not the management's.

Is he, then, in the position of a beneficiary, a recipient of favors, an object of philanthropy? The student cannot entirely dodge this analogy. Even when he pays for his education, he doesn't pay its full cost, and he certainly receives a great many services intended to keep him healthy and happy. And yet, as a citizen in an affluent democracy, as a twentieth-century man with a full quota of human rights, the student is only receiving what the society, it is now generally held, is under a fair obligation to give him. Besides, it needs him for its own purposes, and it needs him trained.

So perhaps a better analogy is that the student is like the protected son in the family, loved and guarded while he is prepared for his future role. In English-speaking countries particularly, the university has in fact been expected to serve some of the functions of a surrogate family, and the student has been expected to submit to some of the restraints of living in the parental nest. But one need only state this analogy to see that it illuminates only a part of the story. All along people have known that, as Mr. Dooley said, at the age when a boy is fit to go to college, he isn't fit to be kept at home. The college has represented the parents, but it has also served the social function of easing the student out of the family and into the public world.

Probably the best analogy is simply that of the apprentice in the old medieval guild. It applies in certain ways to graduate students. The difficulty, however, is that it does not really apply to undergraduates. Essentially, undergraduate students are going through the first initiation rites of the scholarly guild. But they are going through them with a difference. Very few of them go on to full membership in the guild, and no one administers these rites to them with the expectation that most of them are in training to be full-time scholars. What has happened, apparently, is that the scholarly guild has managed to convince the other guilds that its initiation rites are generally useful to everybody else, and not least to the initiate himself. This may be right or it may be wrong, but it means that the college student is not an apprentice in the traditional sense.* We are forced to the conclusion that students are—students! It is a status all to itself, and no other word describes it as well.

This may seem, undoubtedly it does seem, an exceedingly long way around to a tautology. But taking this long way around is illuminating. For most of the odd, novel, or shocking things that are being said about the condition of students in the United States today, and many of the discussions taking place about the re-allocation of powers within universities, depend on the application of loose and unexamined analogies, drawn from other types of social organization, to the structure of institutions of learning.

Thus, to take a doctrine that has achieved growing currency, students are not an "exploited" group. It is possible to say other things about them: for example, that they are in the grip of a punishing and misconceived examination and admissions system that puts too many of the wrong kinds of pressure on them; that they are neglected; that, in many places, they are perversely miseducated; that they are harassed, constrained, and subject to indignities ranging from Victorian rules in dormitories to forced service in the army. Some or all of these are defensible statements. But they do not mean that students are "exploited," if the word means that anyone is profiting from them at their expense. As those who have experienced exploitation know, it usually involves a condition more painful to endure than boring or "irrelevant" classes. When this doctrine is propounded by

---

* This may seem to apply only to students in liberal arts colleges, and not to those in vocationally oriented schools like those of agriculture, nursing, or home economics. But even in these schools, the emphasis is on the mastery of general skills and broad fields of learning, and not on picking up the tricks of a trade.

students in revolt, or by middle-aged people who claim to speak for them, it can encourage, among those who remember the Depression, a feeling that there really is a "generation-gap." And to students who are today trying to rise out of poverty, and to struggle against exploitation, it can give the impression that members of the more fortunate middle class are indeed insulated from reality.

Nor is the larger version of the doctrine of the exploited student any more persuasive. The word "exploitation" has been stretched so that it is used to describe the process by which young men and women, in the best years of their lives, are educated not for purposes of their own, but for the external purposes of an alien social order. The university exists, it is said, simply to provide highly trained labor to the corporations, the government, or the knowledge factories. It is, therefore, an instrument of exploitation, a tool of the military-industrial complex or the one-dimensional consumer society. This sweeping proposition falls to the floor under its own weight. A sharp line cannot be drawn between the individual's "own purposes" and the purposes of the social order. A young man who wants to be a mathematician draws his own pleasure from that profession; the fact that it happens to be a useful profession does not mean that he has been dragooned into it against his will. To be socially useful is not to be exploited, and there is no society, existing or conceivable, which does not demand that its members make some contribution to the collective good.

The difference between one society and another lies in large part in the kinds of exception they make to this general rule, and in the flexibility and scope of their conceptions of social utility. From that point of view, contemporary American society is one of the more, rather than less, generous social orders. Of course, it is also true that in any society there are some jobs to which people have to be force-fitted. They may be useful jobs, but they satisfy no esthetic or moral craving of the individual who holds them. It is hard to see, however, how all such jobs can be eliminated—nor is it even plain that all people want to be stimulated by their work. Einstein said, towards the end of his life, that if he had to do it all over again, he would be a plumber. It was simple, self-respecting work, free from the constant pressure to produce and be "creative." But in any case, college and university education are the best avenues that exist in our society to the kind of work that combines personal commitment and social utility. Of all the groups in society to whom the word "exploitation" is least applicable from this point of view, college and university students would seem to be the most conspicuous.

Of course, the deeper assumption in the charge that higher education is "exploitative" is that it trains students for work which is frivolous or harmful, not useful. The basic purposes of the society are wicked, and its fundamental arrangements misconceived. But we need not examine that very large proposition here. True or not, it cannot be used to indict universities. For the universities are themselves the major centers in which that proposition, in its extreme or more moderate forms, flourishes. They shelter the teachers and students who express and propagate this view of American society. That in itself makes it impossible to denounce universities as unequivocal instruments of the status quo. At any rate, it makes it impossible if one respects facts.

And besides, what system of higher education in the world grants more freedom to students in their choice of studies than the one that now exists in the United States? What system has provided more room for individual variation, more flexibility in programs of study, more diversity in standards and style, more friendliness to eccentricities, rigid and unimaginative though many of its aspects may be? Assume the worst: say that the larger economic system is "exploitative"; say that it chains people to routines and purposes to which they have not consented and which they do not approve. Still, of all the parts of the existing social order, this indictment applies least of all to institutions of higher education. Very few of them fail to offer a viable alternative to the student who refuses to be co-opted into the system: he need merely study music, philosophy, and poetry, and join some protest group. And the chances are good that he will be offered a job by this "exploitative" system which will allow him to go on doing the same things after he has graduated.

Whatever may be wrong with American colleges and universities—and there is plenty—calling them "exploitative" is demagoguery. The war and the draft have changed the objective relation of students to their colleges, and have altered their inner feelings about the experience of educa-tion. These are real but circumscribable evils. Broadside attacks on the university system as such merely lead people away from effective action against these specific difficulties.

In sum, the case for student power cannot be presented as a case against tyranny and oppression. Nor can it be justi-fied on the basis of fundamental student rights. It is highly desirable for a dozen reasons, I think, to give students a larger share of responsibility in the government of the in-stitutions which they attend. But the issue is a matter of practical educational and political practice, not of the rights of man. And this distinction is important. To do something because it is desirable is not the same as to do it because it violates people's rights not to do it. The logic is different, and the consequences are different. Students are indeed members in good standing of a university community. But this community is a hierarchical human organization, based on the premise that some people know more than other people, and that the community cannot perform its tasks effectively unless these gradations in knowledge are recognized in its form of government. Allowing for certain qualifications, the rights which people acquire within this community are earned rights which they have to show that they merit.

This is not an abuse of "democracy." The right of a citizen of the larger society to vote just as the next man can, without regard to hierarchy, is based on the premise that, where the major policies of the State are concerned, where the nature of what is good for society is at issue, only extreme inadequacies, like illiteracy or a criminal record, are disqualifying. The basic reason for this view, according to the believer in democracy, is that there are no reasonably defensible general procedures by which the citizenry can be divided into the class of those who know enough to have an opinion worth counting or an interest worth expressing, and the class of those who don't. And, in addition, majority rule is accepted in democracies only because its range is restricted. Individuals have rights against majority rule, and all sorts of associations exist which are insulated against majority rule.

In contrast, while universities are democratic organizations in the sense that individuals have a broad array of personal rights within them, and that there is a play of opinion inside them which has a massive effect on their evolution, they are not democratic organizations in the sense that majority rule applies to them. For within a university there are acceptable procedures by which people can be graded in accordance with their competence, and grading people in this way is essential to the conduct of the university's special business. The egalitarian ideal does not apply across the board in universities any more than it does in any other field where *skill* is the essence of the issue. To suggest that it should apply is to make hash of the idea of learning. This involves, as the very language of the learned community suggests, the attainment of successive, and increasingly higher, *degrees* of competence. If there is a case to be made for student participation in the higher reaches of university government, it is a case that is not based upon *rights*, but upon considerations of good educational and administrative practice.

To examine this case, it is best to begin by looking at the status quo—the government of colleges and universities by trustees. Does the discussion we have just concluded imply that the present system is a good one? No; but it helps to put the examination of this system in perspective.

The case which is generally presented against trustee control of universities mixes truths with exaggerations. It is true that most trustees tend to be preoccupied with other matters than education, that they are inaccessible to teachers and students, and that a dispiriting number of them have reached an age and station in life calculated to protect them against fresh ideas. It is not surprising, therefore, that professors and students are sparing in the confidence they lavish on trustees. The government of American universities by boards of trustees is not an example of government by the consent of the governed.

However, neither is it an example of tyranny. The powers of trustees are severely limited by custom and law, and by the realities of a university. In any well-established university, trustees normally leave educational decisions to the faculty. One of their primary educational functions, indeed, is simply to provide the educational community of the university—its students and faculty—with protective insulation. The trustees throw their mantle of influence and respectability around it, deflecting and absorbing criticisms and denunciations, and thus guarding the community's freedom. Indeed, it is doubtful that faculties and student bodies, in many parts of the country, could by themselves, and without the help of trustees, successfully defend their autonomy, even assuming that their economic problems could be solved. It is odd that trustees should be attacked as though their presence was in contravention of academic freedom. Their presence is usually a condition for it.

On the whole, indeed, trustees of private colleges and universities probably have a better record with regard to respecting the autonomy and freedom of faculty and students than do boards of regents, chosen by popular vote or appointed by a governor or other public official. Those who call for "democratic control" or "democratic participation" in the government of universities should reflect on the fact that there is a second version of the idea of "democratic control," not less acceptable than theirs, and perhaps somewhat easier to bring into being. If government of a university by private trustees is a form of despotism, why not turn over the government of the university to public control? This is certainly what is likely to happen if private funds are removed, and only tax revenues are available for supporting the institution. Yet most of the evidence suggests that when the general public, through its political processes, exercises control, the autonomy of the faculty and students tends to be put under greater pressure than when private trustees are in control. When a legislature votes the budget, it is usually much more insistent on knowing why Professor X, the mathematician, is sounding off on the glories of Cuba, or how that ragged crowd of students who took over the Administration Hall could ever have slipped through a decent admissions procedure.

The comparison between the record of boards of trustees and that of boards of regents should not, of course, be pushed too hard. In most parts of the United States, public higher education is not now significantly different from private education with respect to the academic freedoms it provides. What is different, however, is the story behind that equal academic freedom. The presidents of public universities generally have to conduct a much severer campaign of public education, and spend a good deal more of their time defending the rights of individuals, than do the heads of large private institutions. If there were no private institutions, this task might well be even more difficult. The private institutions help set the standards. The government of some universities by private trustees is a general condition for maintaining the variety and independence of American education at large.

Still, whether we are discussing boards of trustees or boards of regents, it can be asked whether this form of government is the best form for a college or university. Trustees (or regents) do make educational decisions, even if most of these are only indirect. They allocate resources, do more for one field of learning than for another, and make arrangements affecting the relation of the university to the larger society which bear on the daily lives of teachers and students. Would it not be better if trustees continued to do their work of finding the money, but surrendered the other powers they exercise to the people who really constitute the university—namely, its students and teachers? Obviously, it is doubtful that many trustees would accept this proposal that they should supply the money but keep quiet about the way it is used. Just to see where the argument goes, however, let us imagine that trustees have a capacity for self-immolation not conspicuous in most human beings. Would it be a good thing for them to retire from the scene?

Not entirely. They are the buffers of the university against external pressures. As we have seen, an educational institution requires such protection. Most organizations, furthermore, benefit from having a lay group of critics with deep commitments to them, who are nevertheless not part of their daily operations. In addition, since universities must maintain relations with the surrounding society, they require people on ther board of governors who have interests and experience in that society. And it is always well to remember that, though education, like the law, is in part a professional business, it is also everybody's business. If students have a stake in what happens to them, by the same token, so do their parents and so do lay members of the community. In courts of law, juries are not composed of professional lawyers. On the university scene, the outsider, though he should not have as decisive a place as a juror has, also deserves to be represented.

In part, this function is served by the activities of alumni, and by the presence of alumni on most boards of trustees, and, in principle, it could be served by restricting the "outside" membership on such boards only to alumni. But only in part. Alumni bodies are immensely varied. The main source of private funds for some universities is the alumni, but this is not true for others. And alumni represent only one relevant point of view. There are other "outside" constituencies which a university should serve, and which should be represented on its governing board. In general, the needs of most universities justify the proposition that they should be ruled, at least in part, by people who are not active members of them, including people who have not studied at them.

Yet these same considerations call for change in the composition of most boards of trustees. They call, equally clearly, for changes in the manner in which they communicate with the communities they govern. Boards of trustees ought to have more younger people on them, and poorer people. They ought to have recent graduates, and not only older ones. They ought to have people who have not yet arrived, and not only those swollen with success. The surrounding neighborhood should, if possible, be represented. That is not always easy to arrange because there are so often disagreements about who is "representative" of whom. But if it can be done without creating quarrels that did not exist before, then it should be done. And students and faculty members should either be represented on the board, or should be assured of regular consultation with it.

The case for such changes is not open and shut. Faculties lose some of their cherished independence if they share with trustees the burdens of budget-making, real estate deals, and community politics. The extension of university self-government almost certainly involves the proliferation of still more of the committees which are the bane of many professors' lives; there can come a day when professors—and students on their committees—will curse the people who demanded "democracy" in the university, and yearn for the "despotism" under which they once suffered. Almost certainly, self-government in a university is not likely to be an enterprise in which all will participate. It should not be. A large number of professors are likely to think, and with reason, that they have other and better things to do. A large number of students may have the same idea.

But for those who want to participate, there should be

an opportunity to do so. There are clear advantages to giving members of a faculty the assurance that they are represented in the decision-making procedures of their institution. The sense of distance from the institution's center has had at least something to do with the increasing mobility of professors, their lack of interest in the collective business of their institution, and their orientation towards professional organizations or community problems off the campus. The inaccessibility or uncommunicativeness of administrators is the single largest cause of declining morale in a college or university. The only thing worse, perhaps, is an excessively accessible and communicative administrator who is a simpleton. How to guarantee faculty communication with administrators and trustees—whether this should be done by guaranteeing faculty representation on the board of trustees or by other means—is a question to which answers will vary because situations are variable. But it is difficult to argue against the proposition that trustees and faculty should be in continuing communication, and that this has not been the normal pattern.

The participation of students in the supreme governing bodies of a university raises issues that are equally subtle. Students are inexperienced. They are present on a campus for only a short period, and could serve on committees and boards for only a shorter period. It takes time, on most boards and committees, before new members learn enough to become genuinely useful. Student generations change in their styles and opinions, furthermore, and sometimes very quickly. Students, therefore, bring an element of discontinuity, a shortened perspective and sometimes a short fuse, into the consideration of matters of policy. In educational institutions particularly, continuity of perspective and some sense of the time-dimension are essential.

Finally, student representation on the permanent governing bodies of a university poses a complex problem both practically and theoretically. How do we arrange this "representation" so that it is representative? In a liberal-arts college the problem is manageable. But in a university, with its scores of schools and faculties and its variegated student-body, this is considerably easier to talk about in the abstract than to produce in the concrete. Nothing could do greater and quicker harm to the cause of "student power" than the complaint that the students officially representing their fellows are not really representative of them.

In sum, the idea of student membership on boards of trustees raises as many problems as it seems to solve. Nevertheless, the idea is worth experimentation, even though the number of students who belong to a board, or who sit with it when certain issues are discussed, should probably be small. And there is little question, apart from the formalities of representation on a board of trustees, that machinery for regular face-to-face meetings between students and trustees is desirable. Discontinuity in policy is dangerous, but so is automatic, thoughtless continuity. The long view is estimable, but impatience is useful too. And if inexperience is a handicap, so is experience: it dulls one to novelty. Trustees could learn from students things they will never learn from administrators or other trustees.

In the end, we are discussing not matters of right and justice, but matters of political wisdom. Trustees will not know what they should know unless they mix with the people who can tell them. The community they govern will not understand why the trustees have made the decisions they have, and will not have confidence in these decisions, unless it has its own trusted emissaries to keep it in touch with the board. Faulty communication is the heart of the political problem in the American universities that are today having trouble. Demands for "student power" and "faculty power," so interpreted, are more than justifiable.

ONE MORE WORD, however, is in order. The discussion we have just concluded turns on the distinction between students' *right* to be represented in the government of a college or university, and the desirability, for other reasons, of giving students closer access to the university's important decision-making procedures. The argument has been an argument from desirability and not from rights. But this should not be interpreted as meaning that, within a university, students have no rights. They have rights as citizens of the larger society, which they do not lose when they become members of a higher educational institution, and they also have rights that derive from their special status as students.

The term "power," when used in political contexts, has three levels of meaning. At the highest level, it can mean participation in the actual business of government. At a somewhat more restricted level, it can mean access to the people in authority so that one can advance one's own ideas or interests. At the most elementary level, it means that one possesses certain rights as against those who govern, and that one has what it takes to protect these rights. The most elementary meaning of "student power" is that students have such rights. As citizens, they have rights of free speech and association, and are free to exercise them, subject only to the impact on the rights of others. Similarly, students have the right to petition for redress of grievances; the right to organize legal political actions; the right to live their own lives when off the campus, subject only to the laws and the risks of the larger society. They also have a right, it seems to me, which is increasingly important today, and is too often violated: this is the right to control the use of their academic records.

As for the special rights which inhere in their status as students, they have, for example, the right to invite speakers of their own choice to address their organizations, and to ask the university to provide the facilities required. So far as university authorities are concerned, this is not a matter of educational discretion, but of recognizing a valid claim. Students are captive audiences, forced to hear the opinions of their professors. Their right to free inquiry should imply that they have a right to seek alternative points of view. Other rights of the same kind—for example, the right to due process in disciplinary proceedings when they so request—also belong to them. These rights, as a day-to-day matter, are as important to students as the enhancement of their power over the decision-making functions of a university.

All or most of these rights are recognized, however, in all or most colleges and universities in the country. The live question now is not whether students should have them. It is how far they go. And that brings up the question of the tactics that have been employed at Columbia and many other institutions, ostensibly in the pursuit of student rights.

Chapter Five

The Moral Right
to Impose on Others

THE PROPOSALS that have recently been made for the reform of American colleges and universities have been made in ways that make people pay attention to them. That, it might seem, is a recommendation for the strong tactics that have been employed. But, in the end, one's view on that matter must depend on how good one thinks the proposals themselves are, and on whether they are important enough, and urgent enough, to justify what has been done in their name. Confrontation, hatred, bloody heads, and an atmosphere of fear and suspicion on university campuses are presumably not ends in themselves. One has to ask whether the tactics that are responsible—even if only in part—for such consequences are justifiable. Obviously, the same question can be raised about political tactics no matter where they are employed. But while certain general issues have to be discussed, let us confine the question, in the main, to universities.

A case for the use of such tactics has recently been made by a persuasive advocate, Mr. Dwight Macdonald. In a letter to the *New York Review of Books*, Mr. Macdonald asked people to send money to the Students for a Democratic Society to help keep that organization alive. He confessed that the political line of this student group, which has been a major force in most recent campus disturbances, struck him as "alienated to the point of nihilism." He volunteered his belief that the methods employed by the SDS were often both deplorable and foolish. Indeed, their ideology and tactics could only be justified, Mr. Macdonald admitted, if "a revolutionary situation" existed in the United States, which wasn't the case. Still, on balance Mr. Macdonald thought the SDS was a good organization doing good things, and he hoped people would send it their checks.

Why? Well, something like a revolutionary situation did exist in the United States in connection with two issues, Vietnam and "race-cum-poverty." "The follies and the injustices of the Establishment, in these two cases, are so extreme and so indurated as to make necessary the use of extra-legal pressures. Like, for example, the occupation—or, more accurately, the 'liberation,' as the phrase was—of certain buildings on the Columbia campus to which the students had a moral right, from concrete use and interest, that they successfully asserted against the abstract ownership of the trustees; for a while, anyway."

This is an interesting statement, and a representative one, though it is briefer and wittier than most. Has Mr. Macdonald defined the issues squarely? I think not. Let us start simply with what meets the eye.

Mr. Macdonald says that students have a moral right to

buildings on a campus, based on "concrete use and interest," and that the ownership of the buildings by trustees is "abstract." But if we proceed from Mr. Macdonald's own premise, the students who occupied classroom buildings at Columbia did not keep the trustees out, except abstractly. Trustees almost never enter these buildings. The students kept other students out. What happened at Columbia was that some students prevented other students from enjoying their right, based on "concrete use and interest," to use campus buildings. If rights were abused, it was, in the first instance, students who were the aggressors and students who were the victims. And of course this may have been justified: we have not explored that question as yet. But it is desirable to state the question with exactness.

Nor is this all that invites close and careful attention in Mr. Macdonald's statement. Vietnam, he tells us, and race-cum-poverty are such grievous issues, such extreme abuses, which the authorities have permitted to endure for so long, that extra-legal actions are permissible against them. The example that Mr. Macdonald then goes on immediately to offer of a justified extra-legal action directed against Vietnam, racism, and poverty is the occupation of buildings on a university campus. Is it not possible to ask what connection this action has with the great issues invoked to justify it? Is a violation of students' rights, and professors', the way to strike a blow for peace and justice? Is a university campus the place for a physical confrontation with the Pentagon and the State Department? Is it the place to use coercive tactics, whatever the cause? I do not ask these questions rhetorically: the world has changed mightily, and let us agree not to take anything for granted. Perhaps the answer to all these questions is "Yes." Still, to talk about the struggle against Vietnam and racism, and then to propose the occupation of buildings on a campus as a tactic in this struggle, has at least the appearance of a non sequitur. It leaves us with these questions unanswered.

Mr. Macdonald's statement, however, contains all the essential points of the rationale for the methods of student activists. In essence, it puts forward four propositions: (1) The evils being combatted were extreme; (2) only "extra-legal"—I take it this is a soft synonym for "illegal"—tactics could be effective in reducing or eliminating these evils; (3) accordingly, the use of tactics on a university campus which are extra-legal, and which might even be regarded normally as immoral, is in this case justified; (4) and besides, look at the results: the action worked; people who were originally indifferent are on the side of the protesters; they now realize that these actions were, to use a phrase of Mr. Macdonald's, "the only ones adequate to the historical situation"; so the entire action has the verdict of history on its side, the mark of success on its brow.

It is obviously time that we looked at these propositions carefully.

THESE PROPOSITIONS, in general, raise two kinds of issue: first, the justification of civil disobedience wherever it occurs, and, second, the justification of such tactics on university campuses.

The subject of civil disobedience is beginning to develop a vast literature, and it would be redundant to deal with it at any length here. There are, however, some fundamental issues related to civil disobedience which are immediately relevant. Assuming, for the moment, that we are discussing only nonviolent disobedience, what justifies this kind of violation of the law?

The form in which we commonly put this question

suggests the premise on which we have to begin to answer it. We do not commonly ask why anyone should behave legally. We ask, When is it permissible to behave illegally? For there is always a prima facie case to be made for legality. The law provides a variety of profound benefits: personal safety; an established and dependable way of settling personal and social disputes; discouragement of the violent tendencies in all individuals; preservation of the entire ongoing system of mutual expectation and confidence on which daily affairs depend. These are not small things, and actions that weaken the framework of law endanger them.

However, there are two qualifications that have to be introduced into the statement that there is always a prima facie case to be made for observance of the law. If a legal system provides no effective means for reforming it, the case for staying within the law is weakened. And if the system works in such a way as to deny individuals their basic rights, its claim to be obeyed is still further weakened. The evils involved in this denial of rights have to be weighed against the advantages of maintaining legality. As in the case of the Nazi legal system, it is more than conceivable that the verdict of reasonable and conscientious men should sometimes be against the system.

Accordingly, civil disobedience can sometimes be justified. But the tests that it must pass are extremely severe. The evils being combatted cannot be middling evils. In view of the potential damage that can be caused by challenging the law, they have to be shocking, excessive, inexcusable. The damage they do to the social fabric must be greater than the damage that comes from breaking the law. Moreover, it has to be shown that there are no legal remedies, or that the ones that are available have been used and found wanting.

The converse, furthermore, also has to be shown if the

acts of civil disobedience under examination are to be regarded as genuinely conscientious. A plausible case has to be
made that breaking the law in a particular way will help
remove the objectionable evil; one cannot simply be engaged
in blowing off steam. Still further, it has to be shown that
the consequences of employing such illegal tactics will not
be graver than the consequences of allowing the evil to
continue to exist. Obviously, honest men can disagree about
the persuasiveness of the case that is made; guess and conjec-
ture inevitably play a large part in the judgments that people make about such matters.

But honest men must at least put such questions to themselves and give the best answers they can. This means that,
in practice, conscientious men engaged in civil disobedience
will take actions in which they seek to restrict the bad consequences of law-breaking as much as possible. And this
normally will imply that the action they take will have some
direct and immediate relationship to the evil being combatted. People should not, for example, invade bars and
smash the liquor bottles to show their opposition to com-
pulsory prayer in the schools.

There are some apparent exceptions to these principles,
but they are more apparent than real. Thus, there are cases
when civil disobedience may be justified even though legal
procedures exist which still have the capacity to remove an
injustice. If these procedures have not yet accomplished this
purpose, and, if, because the injustices still exist, individuals
find themselves under a legal obligation to accept an abuse
of their rights, or to engage in actions which assault their
consciences, they have a persuasive case for resisting. The
position of a black man facing elementary indignities which
the law enforces or will not remedy is one example; the
position of a prospective draftee who regards the war in

Vietnam as immoral is another. Civil disobedience may be justifiable, even if legal remedies have not been exhausted, when it is undertaken in defense of one's own personal rights or personal conscience. These circumstances, however, do not relieve a man from the obligation to consider the effects of his action on other people's rights or on general social values. Needless to say, neither do they make what the man is doing legal. At most, they make it moral.

Similar considerations apply to another and very important kind of case. Many acts of defiance of the law are efforts to test a doubtful law. They are intended to force recourse to the courts, and to produce the legal judgment that the law is invalid. The requirement that legal remedies be found and tried before extra-legal actions are undertaken does not apply to the case of a man who seriously believes that he is challenging an invalid law. Such a man is trying to provoke a legal remedy. Of course, the use of this method is subject to the normal questions that should be asked by anyone who is trying to behave responsibly. Is this method, given the circumstances, the one with the least risks to the social fabric? In view of the explosive atmosphere that often surrounds dramatic tests of the law, the question ought to be asked twice. Obviously, however, an affirmative answer can be correct.

It follows, then, that civil disobedience can be justified, but that it takes strong arguments to do so. And this is even truer when the disobedience, though nonviolent, is disruptive. Preventing people from entering a building by interposing one's body is not just a strong case of picketing. It raises questions about other people's rights. Refusing to obey a policeman carrying out his lawful duties is not just an expression of a dissenting opinion. It goes beyond the law, and requires a special sort of moral defense which is valid only in extreme circumstances. Indeed, one of the dangers of the extensive employment even of nonviolent and non-disruptive civil disobedience as an instrument of social protest is that it tends to erode the distinction in people's minds between dissent and obstruction of the law, or between criticizing other people's conduct and coercing them. The effects of this erosion of such basic distinctions have already become visible in our society.

Moreover, there is a final issue that has to be faced. Each man has to make his own judgment concerning the nature of those social evils that are intolerable. But no man can approve civil disobedience in another man's case, no matter how restrained the disobedience is, if he thinks that the cause being served is an unjust one. If members of the Ku Klux Klan were to stage a sit-down demonstration in de-segregated churches, and prevent the services from taking place, this would be, for me, intolerable. The sincerity of the demonstrators would be beside the point: my resentment might be lessened if their behavior was nonviolent, but their crime, in my eyes, would not be excused. And I suspect that, in this attitude, I would have as allies most of those who have found the behavior of student activists, doing not dissimilar things, perfectly excusable.

This is the ultimate practical question which civil disobedience poses. People's consciences differ. If everyone thinks that strong convictions, sincerely held, are enough to justify disobeying the law, we accept violence as the only arbiter, and it is the violence, not of police, who operate under law and against whom we can at least shout "Police brutality," but the violence of lynchers and mobs. Acting on conscience is a fine thing; but a complete conscience ought to engage in some conscientious consideration of the consequences of acting on conscience.

A point at once practical, political, and moral follows from this. Civil disobedience makes sense if it is a way of forcing an issue into the judicial or political arena, where there is a chance that it can be dealt with. It makes sense if it is a way of challenging men's consciences, so that violence is reduced along with the evil under attack. But it does not make sense—it verges on becoming something other than civil disobedience—when it can reasonably be predicted that its consequence will be to take the issue out of the judicial and political arena, and submit it to the test of violence. We then come to a quite different order of issues, as separate from civil disobedience as civil disobedience is from lawful dissent.

Except for those who are absolute pacifists, everyone will recognize circumstances in which the use of violence is justified. It must be plain, however, that all the arguments that restrict the circumstances under which civil disobedience is defensible apply with even greater force to the use of violence. Undoubtedly, there are those who enjoy violence for its own sake, and are prepared to take their chances with it. Arguments about the evils of violence are not likely to influence them. But most people who oppose racism or the war in Vietnam, it may be presumed, are not of this sort, and the evils of violence do not have to be rehearsed to them. However, some of the mounting confusions about the subject do have to be dispelled.

There are points of view about violence which pop up in books, newspapers, and conversation time and again, and which are regularly used to defend a wide range of actions, including the tactics of student demonstrators. Among these points of view—everyone will recognize them—are the following: It is not the students who initiate the violence (except for occasional accidents) but their opponents; Our entire social system depends upon violence, and no one, therefore, is in a position to condemn anyone else for having recourse to it; and, finally, Violence appears to be the only way to get results. These are statements that would probably have seemed quite odd to most people five or ten years ago. It is a sign of the times that they can be uttered today, in many circles, as though they were truisms.

When students make it impossible, through their physical actions, for a university to pursue its normal business, what is the reason for saying that it is not they who have been the initiators of violence on the campus? This position, which is a common one, depends on drawing a distinction, consciously or unconsciously, between *force* and *violence*. Thus, the editor of the *Harvard Crimson*, writing in the *New York Times Magazine*, said last spring:

> Force is becoming a popular student tactic because students are learning that it works. . . . At Columbia, by imprisoning a dean overnight and holding five buildings for more than one week, students have probably ended the Morningside Park gymnasium project and might get rid of an unpopular president in the bargain; they have certainly set people thinking about administrative reform at the university.
>
> This show of force should not be confused with a show of violence. The students do not initiate mass violence; they do not come to their demonstrations armed with guns. The blood that is shed is mostly their own, and is shed only after law-enforcement authorities are called in.

Let us take the facts as stated. Is the distinction a sound one? Obviously, there is a difference between preventing a man from leaving his office, and committing assault and battery against him. Call the first "force," if one wishes, because it shows a certain restraint, and the second "violence." Still, the distinction must not be asked to bear too great a burden; it does not turn what the students did into an act of gentle forbearance. A kidnapper who says in court that his victim suffered no physical harm may persuade the judge to take that into account as a mitigating factor when sentence is pronounced. He is not likely, however, to receive a vote of thanks from the public for exercising such laudable restraint.

I do not mean to imply, of course, that students who hold a dean captive are kidnappers; I don't know the name of the violation of law of which they are technically guilty. But the notion that because one has avoided bloodshed one's actions move inside the pale of morality is still an extraordinary one. Threats, though they draw no blood, can make a man's life unbearable. Intimidation, as every student should know who has suffered it from a teacher, can do more damage than a physical blow. To say that impermissible political behavior begins only when outright violence and bloodshed are involved is to reject distinctions that make up a good part of what we know as civilization. It ignores subtleties of feeling it has taken millennia to develop, and it weakens legal, psychological, and moral controls by which mankind, gradually, with great difficulty, and very precariously, has managed to moderate its behavior. Though offered innocently, it is an attack on man's powers of self-control.

Moreover, to act on this belief invites violence, in the sense of bloodshed. If students hold a dean prisoner, they present his friends with the alternative of acquiescence or the use of greater force. The students, in other words, invite a confrontation of force against force. A usual result of such confrontations is violence. Are those who knowingly risk such a confrontation to be wholly exculpated from the charge of initiating violence? Imagine the case of a man who, with his friends, blocks the entrance to another man's home, refuses to leave after a week's effort to persuade him to do so, and then does not get up and leave peacefully and at once when the police finally arrive. If there is violence, he would not be held free from blame.

The defense of student activists cannot be that they employed only force, and therefore had no responsibility for the violence that ensued. If there is a defense, it is only the old cowboy movie case that the good guys are never responsible for the blood and killing, no matter what they do, because, after all, they are the good guys. The case is that the students' motives were benevolent, and that the principles for which they acted were important enough to excuse what they did. If this is so, they have to be important enough to excuse some complicity in violence.

It is of great importance to recognize the character of the distinction between "force" and "violence." It applies to a spectrum of kinds of conduct that differ in degree. At one end of the spectrum we have force in its mildest form; at the other end of the spectrum we have violence at its most acute. In between, there are all sorts of gradations. Force can be latent or overt, rarely or constantly visible, legal or illegal. "Force" may simply consist in making a peaceful nuisance of oneself. For example, demonstrators against segregationist practices on buses might take prohibited seats, leave quietly when ordered by the police to do so, and then return and do the same thing. By continuing to do this in great numbers, they might shame or exhaust their opponents into submission. This is a coercive tactic, because it involves actions to compel other people to do things they would not freely wish to do. Up the scale a bit farther is the policeman's walking his beat in uniform. Farther along is his carrying his billy. We can then move on to the active hampering of other people going about their pursuits, even though the hampering may not involve blows or bloodshed. The creation of a threatening atmosphere, one in which violence, though not employed, is "in the air," is still closer to the border of violence; then comes the exhibition of guns and clubs, and finally their use.

When do we cross the border into violence? The question is not an academic one. The line has to be drawn. But there is a very large gray area, and people who intrude on it are on shaky grounds when they say, in defense of their actions, that they have been restrained, and have merely used "force." There are all sorts of choices available to those who would use force, some mild and some inflammatory. Those who use force, therefore, must show not only why the use of force was necessary, but why they used the particular kind of force that they did. They must show that, given the purposes which are the presumed excuse, the force employed was not excessive. If it was necessary to seize buildings, was it necessary to seize a dean? And to force an administration to take note of one's complaints, was it necessary to remain until the police came? Those who cry "Police brutality" (as they have a right to do) when there is an excessive use of force against them are under an obligation to ask whether they have themselves been immoderate.

These gradations in the nature of force are also the decisive consideration with regard to the argument that our existing society relies on force and violence, that everyone employs these methods or acquiesces in them, and that no one, therefore, is in a position to point the finger of blame at anyone else. It is true that in American society, as in all societies, democratic or not, almost everyone is coerced in some respects. People pay their bills or obey traffic laws at least sometimes because they fear the application of force against them. It is true, too, that in American society many gross injustices are maintained through unfair laws that are

backed by force, or through the connivance of the authorities with illegality, and, sometimes, as in the case of the
murdered civil rights workers in Mississippi, through outright violence. But to say that this society, taken as a whole,
relies on force and violence, and that all decent law-abiding
citizens share the guilt for this state of affairs, is to ignore
distinctions that have fundamental import for everyday
human experience, and for the quality of human relations,
human feelings, and human conduct.

Force that is merely latent has a different social and
psychological significance from force that is actively employed. Force that is employed subject to strict legal re-
strictions is not in the same genre with force that does not
recognize such bounds. To utter broadside denunciations
of the force and violence on which society depends while
ignoring such facts is to imply that there is no significant
difference between the condition of a man who pays his
taxes because he does not want to go to jail and that of a
man who is afraid to vote because his house may be bombed.
It overlooks the difference—and it is not an abstract difference but something as palpable as a knife in one's side—between living under law and living under terror.

But is it not so, even after all these arguments have been
reviewed, that force appears to be the only tactic that works
if really significant changes are being demanded? The answer, of course, is Yes and No. Sometimes other methods
have worked, but undeniably there are circumstances when
force is the only tactic that works. But even so, unless one
values force for its own sake, the mildest form of force
necessary to achieve the result is alone justifiable. And it is
also incumbent on those who use force to look not only at
the result they specifically seek, but at the other results
they are likely to achieve.

"Force is becoming a popular student tactic," we hear, "because students are learning that it works." But what do we mean by "works"? We are told that, at Columbia, force probably ended the Morningside Park gymnasium project, might get rid of the university president, and certainly set people thinking about administrative reform. This assumes, without argument, that the gymnasium project should have been stopped, that the president should go, and that administrative reform was necessary. And it also assumes much else.

It assumes that rankling divisions within the student body, and rankling divisions within the faculty, inevitably caused when such commotions take place, do not have an adverse effect on a university that far outweighs the hypothetical gains listed. It assumes that independence of mind, freedom of inquiry, reasoned discussion, are not affected by an atmosphere of intimidation, or, if they are, are not important enough to worry about. It assumes that administrative reform conducted under the threat of student reprisal is the kind of reform that will lead to desirable educational results. Those are large assumptions. The conclusion to which one is compelled to come is that force, far from being the only thing that works on a university campus, is one of the things that doesn't work. Those who use it either have no idea what they are doing, or don't care.

So WE RETURN to the four propositions on which the rationale for the methods used by the student activists depends: that the evils under attack were extreme; that only extra-legal methods work against them; that these two conditions are enough to justify the use of such tactics; and besides, it works: the verdict of history already shows that the militant students were right.

Begin with the first proposition: that exceptional methods were in order because the evils being combatted—Vietnam and race-cum-poverty, in Mr. Macdonald's words—were extreme. But there are places closer than a university campus to these evils, where they can be combatted more directly. The university campus is merely convenient, safer, and more vulnerable because force is so alien to its habits and so lethal to it. Would anyone accept the contamination of public beaches or the invasion of hospitals as a legitimate means of protest against the war? Why, then, a university?

The answer that is given, of course, is that universities are in the service of the war machine and racism. But this is not a proposition that can be defended without significant qualifications. If it is true at all, it is true only in part. The universities of the United States have been principal centers of protest against the war in Vietnam and against racist practices. Only in certain of their activities can a connection be drawn between them and these wrongs. If complaint is justified, therefore, it has to be a specific complaint. If there is to be an issue, a concrete issue has to be found, based on a definite and particular connection between the university and the wrongs under attack. And the fact is that, at Columbia, this is what was attempted. Some sort of ostensible connection had to be established between the university and the great evils which, in theory, justified disruptive action. The *specific* issues being fought on the Columbia campus were not Vietnam and race-cum-poverty; they were a relationship to the Institute for Defense Analysis, a gymnasium project, and a maldistribution, real or alleged, of power in the university.

All these issues are issues on which it is possible to be right or wrong, but on which it is overwhelmingly likely that reasonable men will not see eye to eye. In any case, the relationship to the Institute, though it may have been wrong, was an attenuated one, and no member of the teaching staff or the student body was compelled to be part of it. The gymnasium project, involving the building of special facilities for the neighboring black community on parkland principally used by members of that community, indeed had something to do with race-cum-poverty, but it could be interpreted by at least some reasonable and honest men as a constructive, though limited, effort to do something about this problem. The project may have been a bad mistake, and it may have been grossly mishandled, but its utter wickedness had not been evident to all men of good will. And perhaps the university possessed an archaic administrative structure; just the same, that structure was consistent with its being a flourishing university, noted for the distinction of its scholarship and the liberality of its outlook. Are these extreme evils?

If we accept the description of events at Columbia and at other institutions that has been offered even by the most ardent defenders of the student activists, there has been no issue of fundamental student rights (e.g., the right to dissent), no issue of academic freedom, no issue of forced collaboration with either racism or the Vietnam war. These, conceivably, might qualify as issues justifying a forceful defense of basic principles. In fact, however, there has been only one issue of an ultimate sort in these controversies. This is whether a university administration has an obligation not merely to listen, but to follow, the advice of one self-selected group of students.

Moreover, is it true that extra-legal methods are the only ones likely to be effective in remedying the specific evils presumably under attack? The case for this, the second proposition on which student tactics are based is no stronger. At Columbia, the relationship of the university to the Institute for Defense Analysis was already under review by a faculty committee, along with the university's external relations in general. As for the gymnasium and administrative reform, even if one admits all that is said about the remoteness and rigidity of the authorities, it has still not been shown that the seizure of buildings, in contrast, say, with peaceful picketing and outdoor demonstrations, was the only method by which to get these authorities' attention.

When we turn to the third proposition, we are no better off. It tells us that because two antecedent conditions are fulfilled—the evils being fought are extreme, and only extra-legal methods are available—the tactics of student demonstrators are justified. But the two antecedent conditions are not fulfilled. And if they were, the argument would still be a non sequitur. For these two conditions are *essential* to prove that such methods are justified, but they are not *sufficient*. It also has to be shown that the bad accomplished by using such methods does not outweigh the good.

The evidence is on the other side. Noise and public attention have to be separated from concrete accomplishment. Neither Vietnam, nor racial hostilities, nor the distribution of wealth and power in America are in a better condition since these troubles began this spring, and if there has been a "transformation of the popular consciousness" in consequence of the events on university campuses, that transformation has almost certainly been in the direction of greater antagonism towards students, towards universities, and towards policies of toleration for people who "defy law and order." This is a bad score-card. It is a record not only of failure, but of perverse self-defeat. If one wishes to polarize a society, and submerge the hopes for reform, there is no better method than the use of force and violence for no clear reason. It is counterproductive.

Of course, it is true that Columbia and the other universities that have received these blows, to use Mr. Macdonald's phrase, "won't be the same again." And neither will a man who has been in a serious automobile collision. Greater attention should long since have been paid to the need for reform in the system of government of Columbia and other universities. But to argue that the methods that have been employed to get this greater attention were justified is analogous to saying that one should force careless drivers into accidents because it is "the only way" to get them to reform their ways.

It is not easy to exaggerate the fragility of the understandings on which a university depends. Universities have to be so organized that force and violence are never present in them. In consequence, they have fewer defenses, and are peculiarly vulnerable, when these are employed. The reason for this defenselessness is profound. At the heart of a university is a fundamental assumption. It is that ideas should triumph within them, not people's interests or demands, and that ideas triumph by meeting independent standards of logic and evidence, and not by political maneuvers, opinion-management, or the pressure of the mass will. This is an ethical principle, and an extremely difficult one to implement. People in universities often fail to live up to it. But they cannot abandon commitment to it without declaring that the university is not committed to science, to learning, and to the independent criticism of society.

This is the reason why the portrait of a university as nothing more than a system of competing blocs is wrong. Such a portrait is profoundly at variance with the underlying spirit of a university. Its politics, as well as its intellectual affairs, its manners outside classrooms as well as inside them, have to give a place to reason which reason does not have in other domains of human activity. The use of any tactic which substitutes physical pressure or emotional duress for reason is an assault on this basic ethic.

Of course, it can be said that this ethic is myth and facade, a bourgeois illusion, with no relation to the real nature of universities or modern society. That is a very large proposition, and this is not the place to argue it. (Few of those who assert the proposition seem to recognize, indeed, that it needs to be argued.) It is enough to say that without this "myth" and "facade," without this "bourgeois illusion," what would emerge as a "university" is something very different from what our civilization has known and cherished. Anyone who wishes such a transformation is indeed demanding revolution. And if the revolution that he wants involves this rejection of the ethic of reason, then reasonable men should know what to think of that revolution.

The tactic of force "works," it is said. It mobilized people behind the movement for reform; it turned out to be the only tactic "adequate to the historical situation." Those who say this are not thinking about universities but about other things—Vietnam, race, poverty, the wasting of human resources and human beings, the frivolity and meretriciousness of so many of the pursuits that pay off in our society. But to attack these ills, they attack, or acquiesce in the attack on, those institutions in our society of which these ills are least characteristic. And if, in the end, "the verdict of history" turns out to be on their side, it will be delivered by historians whose judgment should not concern us. They will not have the standards which distinguish the intellectual life from Hobbes's "war of all against all." Whatever the case for "student power," the methods that have been employed in its name are unacceptable. No admiration for youthful ardor, no sympathy for the motives of those who used these methods, can obscure this conclusion.

Chapter Six

The Relevant University

YET UNIVERSITIES are not what they can be. They disappoint too many of the best and bravest students in them, and too many sober and moderate students. The extraordinary events that have transpired on American campuses during the past year are mainly due to follies and iniquities for which academic institutions have little responsibility. But these institutions, just the same, have an obligation to make contact with their students, and to recognize the state of mind and feeling in which so many of these students find themselves. The obligation is not an abstract one. It is immediate and practical. Colleges and universities are not going to be able to do their educational jobs if they do not accept it.

This, at the very minimum, is what is meant, I think, by saying that colleges and universities must become "relevant." In their atmosphere and in their curricula they must make connections—they must connect with students' wants and feelings, they must connect learning with conscience, they must connect information with ideas, they must connect the campus with what lies beyond the campus. When students feel uneasy and restive because their education lacks this quality of "relevance," they are not imposing unfair or inappropriate standards on education. They are pointing to inadequacies from which educational systems suffer recurrently, and they are acting as agents of regeneration. The complaint that education is "irrelevant," if true, means that education is not serving as an instrument by which a society can control its future. It is not giving students what they need to make their lives the kind of lives they wish, and to make their society the kind of society they want.

Of course, the problem isn't simple. What *is* "relevance"? A university cannot be asked to harness all its separate departments of learning and all its people to the service of any single vision of the good society. It cannot be turned into the instrument of any particular political purpose, official or unofficial, except the purpose of general freedom and pluralism. If "relevance" means the politicization of the university, then the word stands for the abandonment of free inquiry and criticism, and the negation of individual rights.

Yet even this principle has to be interpreted with care. It does not mean that the individual members of a university must abstain from partisan political pursuits. Nor can it mean that their intellectual endeavors must be free from practical political implications. Such a taboo, obviously, would be impossible to enforce. And to pay it even lip service is to confuse intellectual independence with intellectual retreat. A university should make no collective commitments to outside agencies which dragoon its individual members into activities to which they object. But it should permit its individual members—and, up to a point, it should encourage them—to make external commitments, provided these contribute to the effectiveness of the university as a center of learning and education. Will such work by faculty members and students bring intellectual freshness, social focus, and moral drive to the business of teaching and studying? Or will it deplete people's energies and upset the proper educational priorities? These are the questions that have to be asked when individuals determine the nature and extent of their off-campus activities. They can only be answered case-by-case, and not by ironclad rules.

Moreover, the same questions apply when the outside agency to which the individual makes a commitment is the government. The commitment should be open, not covert. It should not involve the individual in obligations that hamper his performance as a free and independent scholar and critic. It should have intellectual purpose and educational value, and not only immediate practical utility. Apart from such principles, however, there is no catchall formula by which the individual can decide that it is always right, or always wrong, to perform work for the government. The nature and purpose of the work he is asked to do are the key issues, and the individual must turn to his own conscience to decide whether that work is morally legitimate. The university as a whole cannot make that judgment for him.

Unhappily, the entire question of university-government relationships has become a cloudy one. The war in Vietnam and other governmental follies, such as the CIA's intrusions into academic life, have reinforced the natural suspicion of many about entanglement with government. Such suspicion has a prophylactic value. The freedom and autonomy of the intellectual life require it. But it can also be extreme and undiscriminating, and when that happens the intellectual community shuts itself inside its fears, and cuts itself off from the thousand and one enterprises, supported by the government, and often supported only by the government, which are good for universities and useful to the world.

To take a comparatively small example, during my days in government, the Department of State extracted from a reluctant Congress the funds to support a small experimental program called "Diplomats in Residence." The program envisaged giving leaves of absence to ten or twelve senior Foreign Service officers each year and placing them on university campuses, where, at government expense, they could study, renew their contacts with the American intellectual community, and perform such teaching duties as the faculty might ask of them. The idea behind the program was to expose these professional diplomats to insights and perspectives not otherwise available to them, and thus to break down the insularities produced by unbroken service in government.

The program had hardly started, however, before complaints came to me from various and sundry places. Professors argued that this program was an effort on the part of the federal government to intrude an "official" point of view into universities. The argument seemed to me passing strange. The prime purpose of the program was, on the contrary, to intrude an unofficial point of view into the thinking of career officials. And even if the purpose of the program had been to insure that an "official" point of view was represented on campuses, on what grounds could this be declared to be impermissible, so long as the arrangement was open, visible, under the control of the faculty, and not forcibly imposed on the students? To disqualify a point of view *a priori*, merely on the ground that it is "official," is to restrict free debate and inquiry. It simply surrounds Protest with the protections Orthodoxy once had.

Such arguments express not only a strained logic, but intemperate fears. The experience of the past few years suggests that professors and students retain a certain capacity to resist official efforts to persuade them. Indeed, the simplest answer to the charge that the universities of the country have been taken over by the government or the "military-industrial complex" is to point to the usual place where that charge is made—the universities of the country. I do not deny the obvious fact that the government and the economy of the United States receive useful services in return for the money they put into American universities. But one of the services they receive is constant, unremitting, and, very often, extremely scornful criticism. No status quo ever spent so much money to keep itself under attack.

As I write, a British student attending a meeting of the National Students Association in the United States is quoted as saying, "We would rather have no university than a capitalistic university serving a capitalistic function." The remark suggests that he has somehow not caught the magic of subjects—astronomy, linguistics, Greek drama, topology—whose status as creations and tools of capitalism is not immediately demonstrable. But in any case, if there are no universities, what will die is not the established order—capitalist, socialist, or what-have-you—but only the major centers of criticism of that order, and the major hopes for its rational repair.

Yet the fear that contact with government is inevitably contaminating, though it is exaggerated, is not just the fear of ghosts. Universities today cannot be maintained without receiving large amounts of money from the federal government. But the Congress and the executive have not faced up to this need directly. Federal funds have gone to the universities, in the main, to support special fields of research, or to buy the university's services as a contractor performing specific governmental missions. The result has been the unbalanced development of the universities' and the nation's intellectual resources, an undue concentration of effort in fields with military significance, and the substitution of bureaucrats' or politicians' judgment for that of scholars and teachers with regard to educational and scholarly priorities.

This is an issue of basic national concern. But it is one that has to be settled at the legislative level, by finding better ways to support higher education while preserving its autonomy. It will certainly not be settled by expressions of disdain for any relationship between universities and government. Such approaches to the issue are the essence of "irrelevance." They deal with the problem by turning around and looking in the other direction. Universities will not be freer by shunning contact with government. They will merely be poorer—and poorer not only in resources, but in opportunities to do interesting and useful things.

But in the end, of course, the relationship of the university to government is only part of the larger issue—the university's general function or role in society. And no definition of that function is adequate which fails to appreciate that the university is not simply an institution for performing services for other institutions. It has its own needs and rights and dynamics. "Relevance" in the university cannot mean that everything the university does should be morally "*engagé*" in some way or other, or "contemporary" or "useful." To learn detachment, to learn to recognize the limits and ambiguities of one's ideals, is a purpose of education. To take people out of their own time and place, and out of a demeaning and ignorant preoccupation with themselves, is another purpose. And to learn the uses of the useless is a third. The purely speculative, the purely historical, the purely esthetic, enlarge the mind and intensify the consciousness. And besides, in the pursuit of learning, no one knows what will be useful, even in the most practical, bread-and-butter sense of the term.

This is why a university cannot, without question, give students what they think they want or need. Students are not the best judges; if they were, they would not have to be students. A college or university, if it is to catch students and make its educational process take hold with them, must, of course, be aware of their interests and outlook. It must try to find them where they are, and reach them where they live. But it does its job only if students learn to live in larger intellectual and emotional habitations than those in which they lived when they entered. An intellectual education is not a process of "meeting needs," either the individual's or society's. It is a process of transforming needs, both the individual's and the society's.

But the demand for "relevance" need not be an expression of philistinism, puritanism, or anti-intellectualism. It can simply express the student's desire to know what his studies mean. If he is a student of economics, is it enough that he learn the workings of the market? Or should he be invited to study the market as only one possible way of defining needs and allocating resources? And should he be encouraged to measure its implicit morality against a morality he considers rational? If he is a student of physics, is it enough that he learn the intricate and absorbing secrets of the natural order? Or should he be invited to focus as well on the nature of physics as a human enterprise—as a logical construction of the human mind, as an historical phenomenon with conditions and consequences? To demand "relevance" in this sense is to demand more, not less, intellectuality in education. It is to ask that learning be saved from the bureaucrats of the mind.

Nor is a university simply a collection of learned disciplines. It represents an act of faith, in which the society joins, that such things as intellectual discipline, mastery of fact, and refinement of taste are social instruments, resources that can be used to improve the human condition. A university that exists in the midst of slums and turns its back upon them is failing in elementary political prudence. But it fails in more than that. It misses an opportunity to test what it thinks it knows, to enlarge its knowledge, and to give itself a sense of purpose. Colleges and universities have impressive intellectual and moral resources. It is a mistake to think that these will be depleted by being used. In any case, that question is not an open one. They are used. The question for a university administration is to find ways to encourage their being used, not only for the thousand and one scattered purposes to which individual members of the university may lend themselves, but for a few collective purposes which will invite the loyalty of members of the university community as a whole, and will unite rather than divide it.

This, I think, is the kind of reform to which American higher education can now turn itself. I am not sure I see any practical alternative to it. And it is in this context that the reorganization of the government of colleges and universities is best viewed. "Student power" stands for many things, some necessary and desirable, some misconceived, some mysterious. Behind the slogan, however, there are a desire and a belief that are neither misconceived nor mysterious. Students desire to have an education whose character and purposes they can understand. And students believe they would have a better chance to get such an education if they had more chance to take part in designing it, and more chance to understand, through the hard, practical experience of active participation, how the institution to which they belong is governed. This desire and this belief are both reasonable. To want to have something to say about the conditions under which one's community lives is an impulse that educational institutions should wish to encourage. To believe that people learn by participation is a democratic assumption.

The distance our society has moved from acting on this assumption is one of the reasons that sensitive men and women, young and old, find it increasingly vapid. The difficulties American society faces go beyond the issues of war, poverty, and racial tension. Even if our economy were not destructive of natural resources, of the countryside, and of the normal decencies and pleasures of city life, even if it did not pour poisons into the air and water, even if we all enjoyed equally the rights of life, liberty, and the pursuit of happiness, there would still be a large ingredient of a good society missing.

We would have a society industrious, fair, and generous, and capable of prodigies in rational planning. But it would still be acting on conceptions of human needs and potentialities about which the most charitable thing to say is that they are thoughtless. It is not possible to educate people in the tradition of the liberal arts and sciences without creating an articulate minority among them who will respond with dismay to the priorities of existing industrial society, in this country and elsewhere. And it is not possible to give a liberal education to so large a proportion of our population as we are now attempting to do without creating, for this articulate minority, a sympathetic and important audience. The moral and esthetic discontents which have been felt by generations of intellectuals are in process of becoming significant political issues.

Colleges and universities cannot by themselves solve these larger issues, but neither can they ignore them. Certainly, they cannot permit the verdict of aimlessness and tastelessness to be pronounced on their own offerings. They can create for students, and with students, communities in which the direction of things is decided by processes that are apparent and accessible, and in which an individual's experience does not seem to be a visitation on him coming from the secret places of authority. Our colleges and universities, damaged though they have been by recent events, have the chance to produce new forms of education and self-government. Those who disapprove of the tactics of some students cannot let their anger and shock leave them rigid in the face of this opportunity to bring new coherence and excitement to higher education.

About the Author

CHARLES FRANKEL has combined several careers into one. Long a well-known teacher at Columbia, with an established reputation as a philosopher and social theorist, he has also been a successful writer and an active participant in national and international public affairs. He was host of "The World of Ideas," an early foray of the Columbia Broadcasting System into educational television. Between 1956 and 1959 he was chairman of the national Committee on Professional Ethics of the American Association of University Professors.

Between 1965 and 1967, Mr. Frankel served in the federal government as Assistant Secretary of State for Educational and Cultural Affairs. When he resigned his post, Senator Fulbright, on the Senate floor, described his leaving as another of the costs of the war in Vietnam.

Mr. Frankel says of his various activities, "I don't think of them as separate. Philosophy involves reflection on one's commitments, and teaching involves bringing ideas to life. So my interests as a teacher and philosopher flow naturally into practical action, and this in turn plays back into teaching and philosophy."

Mr. Frankel's writing has appeared in periodicals as varied as *Philosophy of Science, Foreign Affairs, The New Yorker,* and *Saturday Review.* His books include *The Case for Modern Man, The Democratic Prospect, The Love of Anxiety and Other Essays,* and *The Neglected Aspect of Foreign Affairs.* At Columbia, to which he returns this fall, he will teach in the School of International Affairs as well as in the Department of Philosophy.